D1716577

Fighting Fire
Fireboats in Action

by Mari Schuh

Consulting Editor: Gail Saunders-Smith, PhD

Consultant: Keith S. Frangiamore, Vice President of Operations
Fire Safety Consultants Inc., Elgin, Illinois

Capstone
press®

Mankato, Minnesota

Pebble Plus is published by Capstone Press,
151 Good Counsel Drive, P.O. Box 669, Mankato, Minnesota 56002.
www.capstonepress.com

1 2 3 4 5 6 14 13 12 11 10 09

Library of Congress Cataloging-in-Publication Data
Schuh, Mari C., 1975–
    Fireboats in action / by Mari Schuh.
    p. cm. — (Pebble plus. Fighting fire)
    Includes bibliographical references and index.
    Summary: "In simple text and photos, presents fireboats and what they are used for" — Provided by publisher.
    ISBN-13: 978-1-4296-1722-2 (hardcover)
    ISBN-10: 1-4296-1722-5 (hardcover)
    1. Fireboats — Juvenile literature. I. Title. II. Series.
TH9391.S39 2009
628.9'259 — dc22   2008026957

Editorial Credits
Sarah L. Schuette, editor; Tracy Davies, designer; Jo Miller, photo researcher

Photo Credits
911 Pictures, 17
Alamy/Danita Delimont/Jamie and Judy Wild, 13
Annapolis Fire Department, MD/Firestorm 30/MetalCraft Marine Inc., 11
Corbis/Paul A. Souders, 7; Reuters/China Daily, 19
Getty Images Inc./Dorling Kindersley/Richard Leeney, cover
Landov LLC/Bloomberg/Robert Sorbo, 5
Photo Researchers, Inc/Peter B. Kaplan, 15
Shutterstock/Gaby Kooijman, 21; Laurence Gough, 9; Rodolfo Arpia, 1

Note to Parents and Teachers

The Fighting Fire set supports national science standards related to science, technology, and society. This book describes and illustrates fireboats in action. The images support early readers in understanding the text. The repetition of words and phrases helps early readers learn new words. This book also introduces early readers to subject-specific vocabulary words, which are defined in the Glossary section. Early readers may need assistance to read some words and to use the Table of Contents, Glossary, Read More, Internet Sites, and Index sections of the book.

Table of Contents

What Fireboats Do

Fireboats work on rivers,

in harbors and out at sea.

Fireboats put out fires

that fire trucks can't reach.

4

CHIEF
SEATTLE

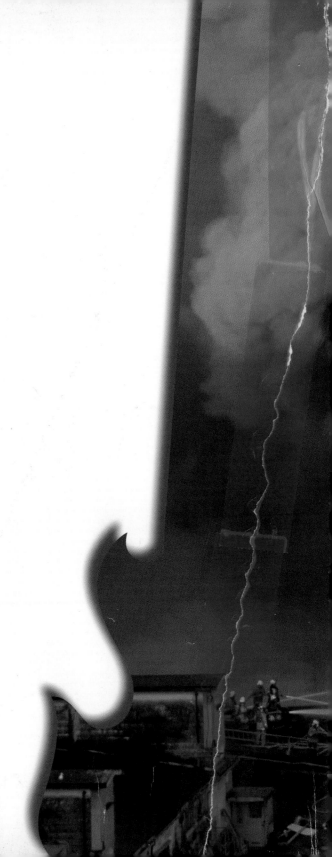

Fireboats fight fires
on ships and boats.
They also put out fires
on buildings by the shore.

FIREBOAT 4

FIREBOAT 5

FIREBOAT 2

On the Boat

Pilots steer fireboats
from inside the pilot house.
The pilot house
is full of controls
to steer the boat.

pilot house

FIRE RESCUE

Big engines push fireboats
through the water.
Bright lights guide
firefighters to the scene.

Firefighters rescue people
on burning ships.
Sometimes other boats
try to help.

Fighting Fires

Fireboats fight fires
with water from the sea.
Strong pumps suck up
sea water under the fireboat.

Powerful pipes called
monitors spray water
on the fire.
Nozzles help control
where the water goes.

Fireboats can spray
thousands of gallons
of water on fires.
They use spray foam
to put out oil and gas fires.

Fireboats shoot water

high into the air.

They put out fires at sea.

Glossary

harbor — a place near land where ships unload their goods

monitor — a pipe on a fireboat that sprays water or foam; monitors can spray gallons and gallons of water a few hundred feet into the air.

nozzle — a spout at the end of a hose or pipe; nozzles direct the flow of water.

pilot — someone who steers a boat, ship, or airplane

pilot house — a room in a fireboat that holds the fireboat's controls

shore — the land along the edge of a river, lake, or ocean

Read More

Butler, Dori Hillestad. *F is for Firefighting*. Gretna, La.: Pelican, 2007.

Minden, Cecilia. *Firefighters*. Neighborhood Helpers. Chanhassen, Minn.: Child's World, 2006.

Internet Sites

FactHound offers a safe, fun way to find educator-approved Internet sites related to this book.

Here's what you do:

1. Visit *www.facthound.com*
2. Choose your grade level.
3. Begin your search.

This book's ID number is 9781429617222.

FactHound will fetch the best sites for you!

Index

Word Count: 148

Grade: 1

Early-Intervention Level: 18